NOTE TO PARENTS

Learning to read is an important skill for all children. It is a big milestone that you can help your child reach. The American Museum of Natural History Easy Reader program is designed to support you and your child through this process. Developed by reading specialists, each book in the series includes carefully selected words and sentence structures to help children advance from beginner to intermediate to proficient readers.

Here are some tips to keep in mind as you read these books with your child:

First, preview the book together. Read the title. Then look at the cover. Ask your child, "What is happening on the cover? What do you think this book is about?"

Next, skim through the pages of the book and look at the illustrations. This will help your child use the illustrations to understand the story.

Then encourage your child to read. If he or she stumbles over words, try some of these strategies:

- **use the pictures as clues**
- **point out words that are repeated**
- **sound out difficult words**
- **break up bigger words into smaller chunks**
- **use the context to lend meaning**

Finally, find out if your child understands what he or she is reading. After you have finished reading, ask, "What happened in this book?"

Above all, understand that each child learns to read at a different rate. Make sure to praise your young reader and provide encouragement along the way!

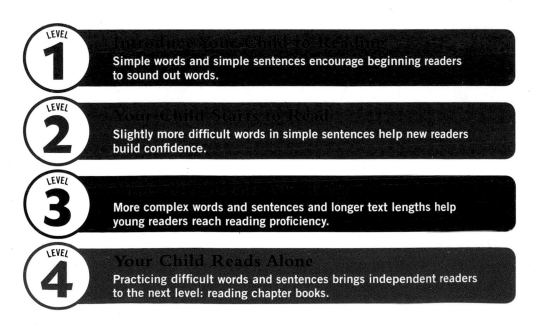

LEVEL 1 — Introduce Your Child to Reading
Simple words and simple sentences encourage beginning readers to sound out words.

LEVEL 2 — Your Child Starts to Read
Slightly more difficult words in simple sentences help new readers build confidence.

LEVEL 3
More complex words and sentences and longer text lengths help young readers reach reading proficiency.

LEVEL 4 — Your Child Reads Alone
Practicing difficult words and sentences brings independent readers to the next level: reading chapter books.

For Steve–of course. —Thea Feldman

STERLING CHILDREN'S BOOKS
New York

An Imprint of Sterling Publishing
387 Park Avenue South
New York, NY 10016

STERLING CHILDREN'S BOOKS and the distinctive Sterling Children's Books logo
are trademarks of Sterling Publishing Co., Inc.

Photo credits
Cover/jacket: © Jane Burton/naturepl.com;
Pages 4–5 (left to right): glass frog © Dirk Ercken/Shutterstock.com,
clownfish © Chris Dascher/iStockphoto.com, oxpecker and zebra © Alta Oosthuizen/iStockphoto.com,
mantis shrimp © John Anderson/iStockphoto.com, archerfish © A & J Visage/Alamy,
bombardier beetle © Johannes Viloria/iStockphoto.com, axolotl © Armin Hinterwith/iStockphoto.com,
basilisk lizard © Ryan M. Bolton/Shutterstock.com, mimic octopus © Stubblefield Photography/Shutterstock.com,
sea horse © huxiaohua/Shutterstock.com, arowana © fivespots/Shutterstock.com, anglerfish © Peter David/Getty
Images, spittlebug © Victoria Martin/Dreamstime.com, glowworm © Dmitry Zhukov/Dreamstime.com,
wrasse © James A. Dawson/Shutterstock.com, green anole © IrinaK/ Shutterstock.com, hagfish © Brandon D. Cole/
Corbis; 6–7: © Chris Dascher/iStockphoto.com; 8: © James A. Dawson/Shutterstock.com; 9: © Alta Oosthuizen/
iStockphoto.com; 10–11: © A & J Visage/Alamy; 12–13: © WaterFrame/Alamy; 14–15: © Carsten Peter/National
Geographic Stock; 16–17: © Peter David/Getty Images; 18: © Mark Conlin/VWPICS/Alamy; 19: © Mark Bowler/Photo
Researchers/Getty Images; 20–21: © Victoria Martin/Dreamstime.com; 21: © B. Mete Uz/Alamy;
22: © NHPA/SuperStock; 23: © Robert Yin/SeaPics.com; 24: © Brandon D. Cole/Corbis;
25: © Dr. Thomas Eisner/Visuals Unlimited, Inc.; 26: © Peter Oxford/Minden Pictures/Corbis;
27: (top) © IrinaK/Shutterstock.com; (bottom) © James Robinson/Animals Animals;
28–29: © Juniors Bildarchiv GmbH/Alamy; 30–31: © Joe McDonald/Corbis; 32: © Chris Raxworthy

ISBN 978-1-4549-0636-0 (hardcover)
ISBN 978-1-4027-7790-5 (paperback)

Distributed in Canada by Sterling Publishing
c/o Canadian Manda Group, 165 Dufferin Street
Toronto, Ontario, Canada M6K 3H6
Distributed in the United Kingdom by GMC Distribution Services
Castle Place, 166 High Street, Lewes, East Sussex, England BN7 1XU
Distributed in Australia by Capricorn Link (Australia) Pty. Ltd.
P.O. Box 704, Windsor, NSW 2756, Australia

For information about custom editions, special sales, and premium and corporate purchases,
please contact Sterling Special Sales at 800-805-5489 or specialsales@sterlingpublishing.com.

Printed in China
Lot #:
2 4 6 8 10 9 7 5 3
03/14

www.sterlingpublishing.com/kids

FREE ACTIVITIES & PUZZLES ONLINE AT

AMERICAN MUSEUM OF NATURAL HISTORY
EASY READERS

STRANGEST ANIMALS

Thea Feldman

STERLING CHILDREN'S BOOKS
New York

Have you ever seen an animal you thought was strange?

These animals do some unusual things.

4

It may seem strange to people, but their

actions help these animals stay alive.

Take a look at some strange animals!

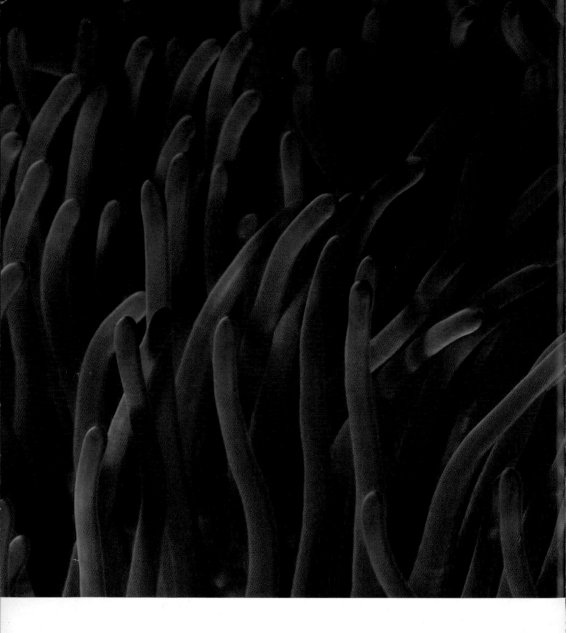

A sea anemone is an animal that
sometimes eats fish.

But it does not eat clownfish.

Why not?

Clownfish attack animals that eat
anemones.

Anemones keep clownfish safe too.

The clownfish eats food off the anemone!

Wrasses are small fish that clean

other fish!

Tiny wrasses eat food that is

on the skin of this moray eel.

This oxpecker bird cleans a zebra's coat.

It eats insects that it finds there.

What a strange way for a bird to get

a meal!

The archerfish sees an insect.

Ready, aim, fire!

It shoots a stream of water out of its mouth and hits the insect!

The insect will fall into the water.

The archerfish will eat it.

A hungry mantis shrimp uses its claw
to smash an animal's shell.

The mantis shrimp strikes hard and fast.

It has the fastest punch of any animal.

Strange . . . and strong!

Glowworms are not worms.

They are insects that make

their own light.

Glowworms make sticky threads

that hang from the top of dark caves.

Other insects get trapped in the threads.

Then the glowworms eat them!

The anglerfish lives in the deep, dark sea.

It has a little light sticking out of its head.

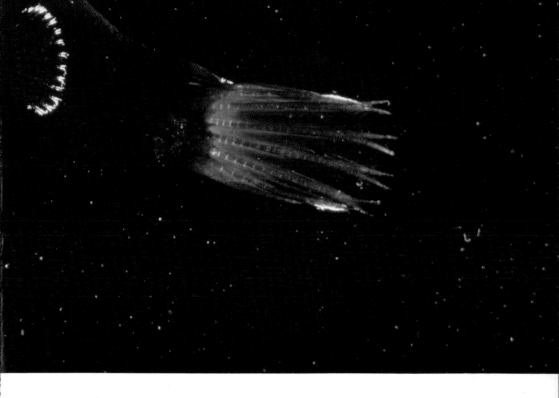

Small fish see the light and swim over
to the anglerfish.

That is how the anglerfish finds food.

Strange . . . and bright!

This male seahorse is pregnant!

He can carry more than one hundred

seahorse eggs in his belly pouch.

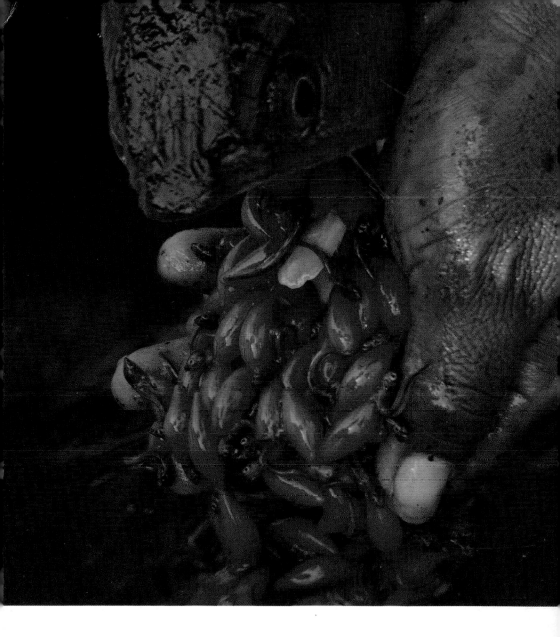

The male arowana carries the
female's eggs in his mouth.
This fish does not eat again until after
the eggs hatch.

The spittlebug uses her own spit
to make a nest for her eggs!

She lays her eggs inside the spit.

Then she leaves.

Her eggs stay safe inside the nest.

The mimic octopus can change its

shape and color.

It can make itself look like other animals!

The octopus does this to keep safe.

The octopus changes its shape.

Which animal does it look like now?

It looks like a fish called a flounder!

How does a hagfish stay safe?

It oozes thick, gooey slime onto

an animal that is coming to eat it!

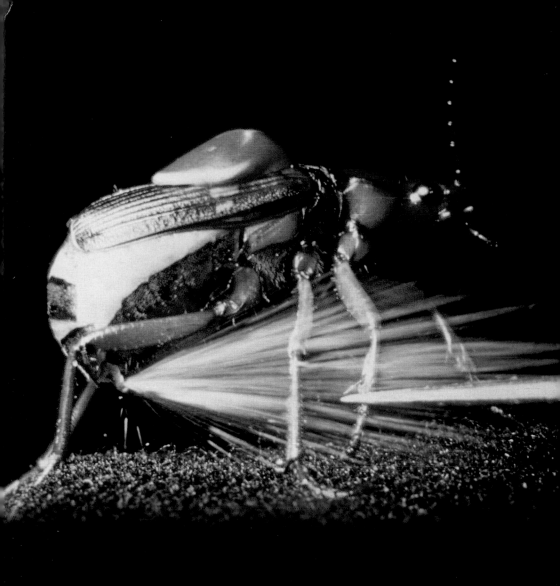

A bombardier beetle sprays a boiling

hot liquid.

It uses this to fight an attacker.

The liquid can blind or kill an animal!

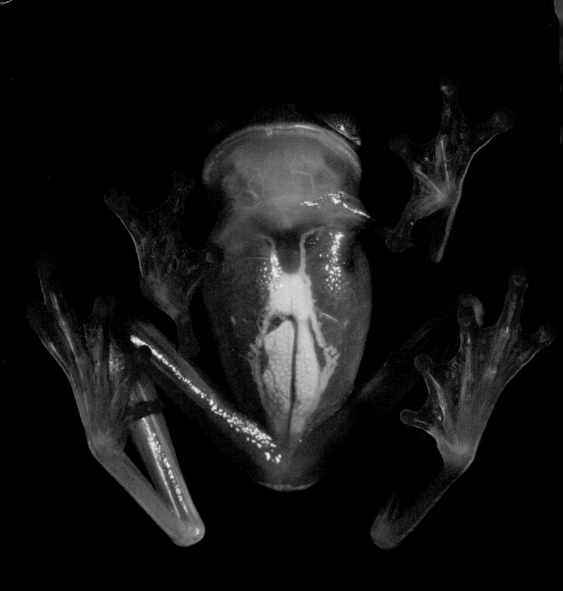

The glass frog has see-through skin

on its tummy.

You can see inside the frog's body!

Strange . . . and very clear!

An animal that wants to eat a lizard
can grab its tail.

But a lizard can break its tail off
and run away.

It will grow a new one later.

Most baby salamanders have a tail fin
and gills that you can see.
When they grow up, they often lose
the tail fin and gills.

But this is an adult axolotl.

When this salamander grows up,

it keeps its tail fin and gills.

It looks just like it did as a baby!

When this brown basilisk lizard

runs away, it runs on top of the water!

It uses its hind legs to move.

Strange . . . and very fast!

What animal do you think is the

strangest?

MEET THE EXPERT!

I am **Chris Raxworthy**, a herpetologist at the American Museum of Natural History. A herpetologist studies modern species of amphibians and reptiles. As a young boy I loved catching salamanders and frogs, and I still remember the first time I held a python; it was at a zoo when I was four. My pet tortoise, Persephone, still lives with me. I bought her in a pet shop in 1979. While I was at university in London, England, I studied zoology and learned about many strange animals, like the ones you've just read about. Working at the American Museum of Natural History means I am always learning new and exciting things about our natural world.

My research includes exploring little-known tropical forests in Madagascar, Africa, and in the Indian Ocean. I look for new species of reptiles and amphibians, and I describe where and how to find them. Sometimes we walk for several days to reach a study area. My favorite reptiles are chameleons. More than half the world's species of chameleons are found only in Madagascar.

When I am back at the Museum, I use my field results, the research collections, and our laboratories to look at the form, genetics, and geographic locations of the animals I study. This helps us to protect rare species and better understand how these species evolved and what habitats they need. I also teach students, work on exhibitions, such as our exhibition *Frogs: A Chorus of Colors*, and help make all kinds of books, including this one!

AMERICAN MUSEUM ᴼꜰ NATURAL HISTORY

EASY READERS

LEVEL ONE

LEVEL TWO

The **American Museum of Natural History** in New York City is one of the largest and most respected museums in the world. Since the Museum was founded in 1869, its collections have grown to include more than 32 million specimens and artifacts relating to the natural world and human cultures. The Museum showcases its collections in the exhibit halls, and, behind the scenes, more than 200 scientists carry out cutting-edge research. It is also home to the Theodore Roosevelt Memorial, New York State's official memorial to its thirty-third governor and the nation's twenty-sixth president, and a tribute to Roosevelt's enduring legacy of conservation. Approximately 5 million people from around the world visit the Museum each year. Plan a trip to the Museum, home of the world's largest collection of dinosaur fossils, or visit online at www.amnh.org.